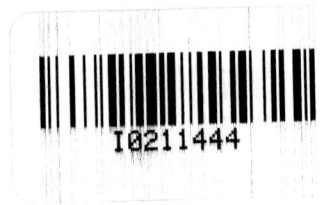

BULLHORN HIGH WIRE

BULLHORN HIGH WIRE

MATTHEW NIES

RESOURCE *Publications* · Eugene, Oregon

BULLHORN HIGH WIRE

Resource Publications
An Imprint of Wipf and Stock Publishers
199 W. 8th Ave., Suite 3
Eugene, OR 97401

www.wipfandstock.com

PAPERBACK ISBN: 979-8-3852-2324-4
HARDCOVER ISBN: 979-8-3852-2325-1
EBOOK ISBN: 979-8-3852-2326-8

06/19/24

This book is dedicated to the memory of my friend and mentor, Larry Woiwode.

CONTENTS

Part 1

BEYOND

Part 2

DAKOTA

Part 3

PAUSE

Part 4

STEEL

Part 1

BEYOND

BULLHORN HIGH WIRE

"Bullhorns! Bullhorns! Get your bullhorns!"
A corner man shouted for the free give out
Amid a din of new Horseshoe power.
Everyone was taking them
And surveying the shiny toys
That weren't toys, or at least they could be more than toys—
"Boredom blockers,
Social boat rockers,
Self-importance,
Miscellaneous unimportance,
More information that you can handle,
Akin to fireworks and a Roman candle—
A new light bulb for a new century!"

But you put yours down. "No bullhorn," you say as you start
    across a high wire.
No tethers tie your moccasin feet to safety. And you do it without
    alerting the masses.
The masses look up anyway
To see you live or die in Niagara mists.
And you walk.

MARVEL UNIVERSES

There's a universal Marvel thread "to each, to each,"
that is to say that unspecified specific universes
depend on the sacrifices of others
to prevent unfolding chaos
like unnoticed death. Do you follow
that Thanos or Ultron or spectacular unfettered likes
could destroy us and them, that it's up to us
to ensure our legacies and seemingly
countless unknown lives? I've assumed
Black Panther was ours (or Wakandans'), Iron Man, Captain
    America,
Spider Man, X-Men—
that even other-world god heroes like Thor and Star-Lord
hero-ed what was theoretically accessible.
But the dirt of the universe—the bony, brawny, anchoring canon
    stone—
is that we're just *one*, and our failures could spill, and will,
beyond the beyond and into incomprehensible realities
where our doom can share itself like tidal waves.
We shadow-watch in dim caves deluding that
we are all; and so we fall. WE FALL.
That's the gist, I read and see, of Marvel universality;
and I believe even comic books, or maybe especially comic
    books,
can convey a special wisdom that sticks with you—
that our lives are not absolutely disconnected.

APOLLO ROSE

Apollo rose,
launched by Saturn's fury
from his earthly chains—
gravity defier—
three astronauts crewing
to a well-known unknown celestial body.

Shuddering
violence—
tremendous belly fire
roaring like some dragon—
slowly jarred the
skyscraper
rocket
from his post—
building
desperation, tallying
speeds of thousands of miles per hour,
hundreds of thousands of miles to go.

He was masculine and feminine energy,
fifty years ago,
lifting hopes and dreams—
and three men—
beyond grasping atmosphere fingers
to Luna's bosom.

Where have you gone,
Apollo—
locked in the dreams of our
fathers and grandfathers,
mothers and grandmothers,
leaving heaven to machines?

We chose to go
to the moon
because it was hard—
reveling in the deed's glory—
to be the first,
and still only,
to send our boys
to walk
its surface—
their footprints still imprint
the gray dust.
Our daughters

aim to return,
but not with Apollo—
Saturn silenced too—
forever fettered flotsam,
daring dreamer
of our dreams.

BATTENED HATCHES

Soundless space flight,
Furious foray away from green men—
He was a blue man—
Onboard a galactic cruiser
With laser cannons to port and the rushing,
Approaching green men in their cruisers.
Battened hatches shook
As the blue man's escape was cut short
By a command ship's tractor beam,
Whisking his ship trembling into its hull.
There would be a boarding party breaching;
He clutched his pistol and eyed
The rear battened hatch. It exploded.
He fired into the fury
Again and again and again:
Successive shrieks and moans.
Then his pistol overheated;
It burned his hand. He tossed it aside.
With unintelligible oath,
He charged into the breach—
His last charge.
Gurgles and grunts and guttural screams
Mixed with cannon fire,
With laser blasts,
With fisted thuds and breaking skeletal structures,
Then silence.
The green men carried the blue man
To his stolen vessel and threw in his limp body,
Released hold,
And the ship with the breached battened hatch
And lifeless crew floated into space.

READING "EVENING HAWK"

It might be easy when you're worn and drawn out and tired
To look at a blank page,
Or more likely a screen,
And despair of what there is to write.
And then you read a poem like "Evening Hawk"
That cuts through time and history
With graceful wings.
You realize it's just fog;
There really is more,
An unimagined infinity,
And it's beautiful.

GLASS CEILING

Valid wake of earth pretending
To be heaven, yes, we're riding fast
For your happiness and unrelenting
Smiles. Quell at the breaking of the glass.

GOING TO A MUSEUM IN RAIN

Gray day—
as I imagine a perfect sweating swath of coffee would be while
bar-window-watching wet wanderers under umbrellas
and crisp cars peeling spray-wet tires through streets
singing like thick paint as it's rolled onto a wall—
and we zoom through the gloom to the tune
of a song sung, only renewably as children can, for a hundredth
    time.
We're going to a museum, for a hundredth time, to
our favorite domed home of bones and the bones of bones—
objective weave of the fabric we're woven from—as if some
tide pulls us into studying fantastic displays, the rain and the day
in balance to the challenges of just getting there.
When I was young, I believed heaven's rhythms could heal
like a hot bath and chicken soup;
now, it's all I can do to keep kids dry on a drive to science's
    exhibition.
And then we arrive, eyes wide and riveted in the joy of joy,
the awe of awe, of precipices glimpsed and delighted in.

The Smithsonian National Museum of Natural History. Photo by James Di Loreto, Smithsonian Institution.

SAND SCULPTURES

How true a trope, too tried cliché, is proved
By easy understanding—so seashore sand,
Compact and soft, avails a *perfect* try
To show how life, in elemental rocks,
Constructs its castles, builds impressive walls;
But time unleashes tides that decimate
All plans; yes, flattens monumented sands
Which, lone and level, stretch, and trimmed in foam.

WHAT IS THAT YOU SING, MY SON?

"What is that you sing, my son?
What new song is passing through your lips?"
"A tune I heard in the village, papa,
Sung between strikes at the smith's."

"What were you doing at the smith's, my son?
What business drew you there?"
"A new shoe for my horse, papa,
For he'd lost one in the village square."

"What happened in the square, my son?
What dislodged your horse's shoe?"
"An uneven stone struck fast, papa,
As we raced down the avenue."

"What have I said about racing the avenue, my son?
What drove you to disregard my advice?"
"A boy insulted you, papa,
And I could not let the slander lie."

"What is wrong, papa?
Why do you turn away?"
"Nothing is wrong, my son,
I am proud of how you managed in town today."

AN INTERVIEW

What is an interview
But a spotlight?
Flaring scrutiny,
And we see ourselves across the table
Or on the other screen.
It is a dream.
Self-identification and pride of sailing through the fog
Complement intoxication,
And it is all about me
Except if it is all about you.
That is an interview.

A HANGING

It was an old gallows. We were callow young men
Gathering the captured for execution.
Rain began dripping fire
Into the muddy mess of it all.
We hanged them quietly,
One after another,
Until the last.
He asked if he could speak before his death.
Our wicked captain smiled
And said "yes." We grumbled.

The lone soldier cleared his throat.

"I'll not long delay your dinners. Intent
Brings us beyond our vision, to battle
For glory in defense and conquest.
Pro patria mori, we say, a story you prattle,
Too, to enlisters. What force we wield yields only to death, as I
    prepare to see.
All my childhood, I was ever too young to know the meanings
    beyond.
And now that I am old enough to fight,
I miss my innocence. We are innocent as wolves,
Helpless as lambs, and caught in gunpowder disagreement.
In another life, we could be countrymen, instead of staring hatred
    across unmarked fields."

We were all dumb when he was done.
The executioner pulled the trapdoor lever.
He died like the rest.
But we couldn't take his body down,
Not that day.
So we let him hang in the rain.

We watched his corpse weather the storm.
Word came after that war was over,
Peace brokered a day before.
We cut the soldier down and buried him
As we buried them all.
And then we went to our homes of unmarked fields.

ON A COLD WINTER'S NIGHT AND AFTER SERVICE'S DAN MCGREW

On a cold winter's night,
A howling breeze knocking with a cudgel of snow,
Mike's saloon door crashed open. Into the light
Walked a fellow, yellow and green and old

With wry smiling eyes and tattered clothes.
"Hooch!" he cried, and bellowed "All you've got!"
Then he cursed and laughed and drew a giant gold
Nugget from his breast. "There's enough there for the whole lot—

Drinks for everyone!" Violent cheers, especially from Mike,
    accepted
The unexpected gift. Strangers surrounded the miner
With friendship, and they were all ears on his prospected
Poke. He drank a first rye and shouted "nothing finer!"

Then greeted another and another in haste
While wetting his weathered lips with the only tincture that can
    cure
Long night loneliness and cold, and sometimes not even that. He
    chased
Another and another and his eyes turned pure

Fire and brimstone; his homely laugh began to growl
And he licked the hard stuff and licked it again.
Then he swore like nothing before. "The fowl
Air is fowler for your breath," a rascal said. Then

Outlaw Bill and his hands kicked down the door, pistols raised,
And exploded shells into the drinking, fowling brute.
His body crashed unnatural, with withering hate
For tundra faced and the warmth of the saloon.

The liquids poured, whether drunk or from the heart. Not a
    lawful soul
Moved. "The poke," Bill said, and an awful gang man obeyed and
    stole.
Outlaw Bill cursed and laughed and held it aloft. "See who steals
    my gold!"
They disappeared. Salooners returned to drink, but none as
    before or half as bold.

LONGFELLOW'S "SNOWY DAY"

"The day is cold
and bright
and icy.
It snows,
and the whipping wind is feisty."
Longfellow looks up from a crackling fire
to a cross-braced window across the room
and through to a corral fence outside, boards and wire
bare to a blizzard swirling snow.
He shakes his head
And dips his eyes, surprised that life could be so cruel
In its seasons. The fire cracks again, and Longfellow starts.
"Rain," he says, "it should be rain."
And he smiles and turns again to write.

LIBRARIES

Kids see bigger,
Beyond just facts and figures,
But certainly those, too,
With a natural view
A little closer to life's fabric.
Can you re-imagine magic
And follow threads to a land of fairy tales
To take home? Generational "Oregon Trails"
Give way to aisle-readings
That slip time to studying
In the light of floor-to-ceiling windows
Even intensified by snow.
Knowing what we know yet surprised
To find unexplored tundra, we prize
Not simply stories but masterpieces,
Grand adventuring romances
In libraries reborn as central crowns
For a pantheon of downtowns,
And hidden jewels punctuating well-laid plans—
Gifts beyond the void of Time's play sands.

ON CHATGPT

There's a complex, learning "intelligence" that sources
The way we think in a blink.
It's one of thousands in a month,
Though the most noted,
To automate to create.
We're setting tables to outsource
At least the most mundane attempts
To breathe through proverbial ink,
And yet, I have to set the table for a meal,
Because no algorithm can.

Frying eggs and sausages with pancakes
On a Sunday morning may be mine
Until the end of time.

I'd like to see AI creators outsource my daily dose of cleaning;
I'd be fine with letting go of tidying up after my family
And not having to prep bikes and meals—just ride and eat.
But that's not the deal; we take our highest arts and give them
    away,
While we must still take out trash.

I don't begrudge AI; I could do with more.

THE LEGEND OF BLAKELEY, ALABAMA

Prologue
Blakeley, Alabama, briefly bigger
Than its neighbor Mobile,
Now sits a ghost town state park. Yellow fever
Epidemics decimated and nearly cleared

The town. Civil war finished the job. Before
Demise, some say its fate was prophesied
By a slave, sold in the town square. Lore
Has a way of burrowing, and I,

A boy at first hearing, am old. Whispers haunt
The once town, now heath, empty trees, and swamp.

***

"Sold!"—final bid, final buy
Under a too-hot spring sun, cloudless sky.

The buyer, a farmer called "Beau,"
Had stood tall and bid though

None other dared. The mean spit seller
Pulled him aside. "I won't lie, you're

A brave man or a damned fool. Do you know
Who you've bought?" Beau

Raised his hand and paid the man,
Then turned to get his. "He should understand

That's no ordinary—." The seller never left town.
Beau strode confidently around

The auction house to fetch his body:
Tall man, big hands callused, swarthy

And bright-eyed—a beautiful, strong specimen,
"A credit to his race," two women

Too-easily said in passing, Beau thought. He leered.
But looking again, even he, looks so often jeered,

Begrudged he was a fine man, though slave.
"Is there a name I should call you?" Chains

Shivered. "Call me Habakkuk. Violence! Here
At the mouth of many rivers, violent cheers

Will usher final falling of proud stars, proud bars—
Injustice and inhuman plundering. It will be a war

And children of Abraham will see its end in freedom.
Even here, weeping and gnashing of teeth, but the kingdom

Will be bettered by the rooting out." The deep
Clear words struck Beau dumb. Habakkuk breathed

Deeply as he had as he spoke, tight, bare chest
Swelling and falling as it glistened. "We'd best

Get home," Beau stammered. They passed
A thick, towering oak tree. "That's

Where they hang folks." Habakkuk surveyed
The gray-brown limbs, moss surfaced,

Casting a shade pall on the square. He broke
The air: "The oppressed will have hope,

But not until their oppressors have been broken.
Here, in this square, in the shade of this oaken

Instrument of death, many will plead for life.
But life will not be found. It will be the first time

Fever will rage. It will not be the last."
Beau hit Habakkuk, yet lashed,

The prophet slave did not flinch. He smiled.
The embarrassed farmer led with erstwhile

Determination to the docks. Beau explained
How he was there principally to sell grain

And had, while waiting, decided to watch the slave
Sale. "You were a price I couldn't refuse," he said.

Habakkuk stared into steaming Mobile Bay.
"Ships sail unmolested into this port. But the day

Will come and soon when they will not dock
Here. A second rush of fever will crush the rock

On which this house is built. And the rocks, which cry
Out for justice, will hear reply:

'Rest from your indentured weight, from the tyranny
Of men selling men. The evil of your ports will be

Silenced. Surely, your sister city will prosper;
You will be lit only in her glow and watch her

Grow while you sleep unsullied.'
And these rocks shall sleep."

Beau uneasily took his slave to the saloon.
"I'll be back," Beau said. "I'll be back soon."

Habakkuk's former owner saw Beau at the bar
And bought him a drink—"Whiskey, from the jar.

How's your new slave?" Beau grinned. "He says
He's a prophet, been prophesying doomsday

For this town. He says yellow fever and war
Are coming." "Do you believe him?" "Are

There reasons to believe?" "He's prophesied
Before. It's all come true." "Is that why

You sold him?" The seller nodded. "Before you bought
Him, he told me I'd never leave town. I thought

He was crazy. I've always thought he was crazy.
But now I'm not—" he wretched, yellow and bloody

Mucus pouring from his mouth. He fell convulsing
To the floor. A mad panic of men carried

Him across the street to the doctor's. Beau
Stopped at the saloon steps. "Before I go,"

Habakkuk said, "I will speak once more.
Here, there will be a great cry such as has not before

Been cried, nor shall there be another like it.
In the church will descend unholy quiet.

Poetic demise strikes deep and full
At hypocrites of history—yes, even defiant souls.

Crying mothers' comfort will be their own death,
And no longer will the living covet breath.

Oh death, where is your sting?
Here, here in the town of Blakeley.

The census-takers return weeping:
'Who can stop the horsemen's racing

Steps? Who can stay God's judgment?'
For a third time, a final time, lament

Will rise for the sick, grief for the dying
And the dead—a third and final time."

Habakkuk rose chainless and walked
Away through confused streets. Beau watched

The beautiful man. That night, he was
Found sick in the street. He never left town.

INTEGRAL

Do not despair
    of your small place in every thing of all.
We occupy only,
    and yet marvelously,
Our lives of rippling breaths in effect of eternity.
You are that jewel mortar of
    endless existence,
As an ocean could never be without each
    water drop.

CAN YOU WRITE IT

Without commas or capitals,
periods or parentheses; rolling like spiders' webs
unavoidably sticky; jutting like spine trees canopied
too close to count each individually
and color crashing like waves of frozen lightning
down slopes of a shell where earth
could not keep itself from reaching for the sky;
cringing that same sharp pain
your reading voice contains like scalpels
in a tossing-ship surgeon's sea-sprayed and shaking hands—
can it still be grand in just its words?

FOR INDEPENDENCE DAY

America, I love your dreams
Blood-written into foundation;
And though we cringe at some histories,
Never have men cast a better, kindred vision.

MELODRAMA

My heart is broken,
    I see the pieces scattered here and there,
And all my focus
    Is on the bleeding—*my* life, unfair.

If I could but fix my heart,
I would have long ago,
Each new day replete with thoughts
Chilling summer rains to snow.

I see your lips lingering again in memory,
Pleasingly puckered and pleading
For reply. And I replied coldly,
Strategically melodramatic without planning.

My heart is broken,
    I see the pieces scattered here and there,
And all my focus
    Is on the bleeding—my life, *unfair*!

BURNING BUILDING MEN

We need burning building men
To walk the streets with worthy confidence
Of our capricious commonwealth, men
To charge catastrophe seeking to upend

Society, *falling bricks and fire be damned.*
No glory except in deed,
These are the men we need:
Bold champions of faith
In heroism, commonplace
And unflinching saviors
Even of complete strangers
Bearing standards of an ideal man

Born in and through disaster furnace heat.
Celebrate the everyday paladin
Who shirks praise. Who knows when we
Might depend on burning building men?

THE MAKING OF A MAN

There is the making of a man,
In breaking, shaking fury storms,
Bone-rattling waves that gnash at their
Gnarled black cliff overlords cutting ocean mist.
Wood stumps gash soft ground and there's no sound
Equivalent for steel-smacking volcanic eruptions
Reshaping the earth's crust and atmosphere.
Then, in all the smelt, a man appears.

TO THE BOLD

Poor pulse-reader, leader of a light brigade
Soldiered by some few romantics
Charging valiantly ineffective into a fray
Of darkening war with doom at its precipice—
I pity you with envy
For your friends and enemies.

Part 2

DAKOTA

MENDING FENCE AND AN ODE TO ROBERT FROST

Wake of snapped disorder, loosed boughs, rotted T-posts—
Unlovely cuts for miles careless of countryside;
And gnarled by Nature for audacity as anything exposed;
And necessary divide between farm and ranch.
No one watches the subtle degradations,
But in spring we find even year-old fences compromised.
Whose barbed wire barriers they are must mend
Before livestock can be loosed to graze.
You know the proverb about good fences and good neighbors,
And who is one's neighbor;
And this is never truer than when there are cattle to curtail
From ripening crops; it takes but a few to chew
Holes in well-laid plans—trampled rows a more
Destructive outcome of meandering kine.
I have propped up miles of neighborly infrastructure—
Spliced and stretched, pounded new posts, untwisted scrambles—
And put up new to halt the wandering calves
And ensure congregated cows in summer heat,
With their rumps together and tails whisking away flies that
    never fly away,
Do so on the right side of the fence.
Still, there are some that do not heed a fence,
And use their bovine strength to break
Or squeeze through
Or jump to greener grass;
These must be loaded and sold;
They cannot be reasoned with.
One can imagine endless grass dotted by bison
Which ruled this boundless empire until
Industrious like Roosevelt and hopeful homesteaders,
Seeking enrichment from sod quartered and sectioned,

Drove cattle to fatten on native prairie.
Distinguished, multiplying neighbors began to hem in their
  husbandry,
Traditions we honor by planting rusting steel.
I have wondered as I have worked if fences were necessary,
If there were superior barriers to decorate our shortgrass steppe,
If it is so important to be a good neighbor,
If cows can be reasoned with.

A fence runs through a flooded slough near the Nies farm in North Dakota.

ROUGHRIDER WOIWODE

Portrait of Larry Woiwode for North Dakota Theodore Roosevelt Rough
Rider Award, by Vern Skaug, 1992.

Theodore Roosevelt rode rough,
if he had to,
And even reveled in the riding.
North Dakota may not have actually made him President,
Though he said it did,
And it was incubatory revelation and beauty,
Soul balm rebirth,
a springboard rebound for his boundless energy.
Larry Woiwode doled out tough advice,
If he had to,
And even drew out the best of a piece and its author.
He may not have actually made me a writer,
Though I'll say he did,
Providing a catapult of wisdom,
Practical grit,

A springboard launch to belief and determination.

Is that remarkableness why Woiwode won North Dakota's award
    or why Roosevelt's name was attached to it?
The vapors of themselves and who we conceived them to be
    endure,
Men beyond our suppositions, greater
Than we knew,
Than we really knew.
How well do you know such men?

Wakes of extraordinary people are
legacies,
memories,
words,
And they're people who cherish and live through
The true sense of what they stood for.
Woiwode was one of four "Rider Writers"
(Erdrich, Hill, L'Amour the others)
That North Dakota commemorates
In its Art Deco Capitol building,
And *he* wrote the bios of *two others*—Harold Schafer and Sister
    Thomas Welder.

Should we slip into lyrical embellishment?
He's still there, his life like any of ours in a way,
Inspiring beyond, and we can hear him speak still.
A job well done is in itself whole.
No award, however deserved and fitting,
Can draw out enterprise, nor contain success.
But we mark as one a distant point
To guide us through that terrain which lies between,
As Roosevelt did in North Dakota
In the springing of renewal,
As Woiwode did in North Dakota
In the passion of resolve.

PRAIRIE METAPHORS

Billowing grasses, wind whipping past us and
Walt Whitman[1], too, sailing on a ship over the gale steppe
steeped in green mist and the star spectacled black
of pure nights set winter-white and brilliant.
Willa Cather[2] whispers our attention to harsh jewel lights
  burning eternal, northern bright
and so moon-like—bathed in waves—that we mistake it for youth
  and hope,
missing what is there for straining to find what is not there.
It is metaphor for the eyes and ears, very tears of God
rising monumental, as Larry Woiwode's[3] words,
in crowning tented buttes above wrinkled, ironed sod
slipping and shod through the years
with third-day creative command.
We can hear the iron, too, in Carl Sandburg's[4] throat
As though he wrote onto our guts the ruts of section lines and
  gravel roads
Arrow straight through black loam that Grace Sperling[5]
Stoops the sky to kiss. William Cullen Bryant's[6] English is amiss
To claim our lonely wilderness that John Hay[7] deems
Rapt in a dream of God. So then, is it very odd that David
  Solheim[8]
Cultivates a continental carapace, a fulcrum
Just in need of a lever long enough?

1. Whitman, "The World Below the Brine"
2. Cather, "Prairie Spring"
3. Woiwode, "Thanksgiving 2022"
4. Sandburg, "Prairie"
5. Sperling, "The Peace of Prairies"
6. Bryant, "The Prairies"
7. Hay, "The Prairie"
8. Solheim, "From the Heart of Turtle Island"

That is the stuff! The rub of myths and legends lies in similes
and metaphors, in commonplace finding a pantheon place
in Olympus or Asgard or some other great paradise,
alive with unfathomed gaiety. The prairie has all it needs.
It does not care for itself,
It fires and digs and pummels with ice and snow,
And it wraps itself in fury,
and yes, too, in quiet mist and summer days,
days we call perfect in the clouds,
With proud dew and opportunity riming in its own way.

Section line and fields near the Nies farm in North Dakota.

FOR ROBERT BLY

We were indecent men once,
disemboweling sanctity at any cost
with our whittled sticks like bronze,
and strung to balance all or naught.

Robert Bly had a poem-line about sticks
straddling waterfalls, and that's salt
of a God-hunching-over-a-pistachio-truth. And quick
currents really fly; they don't halt.

TO FARGO AND BEYOND

Tapered tufts of stratus
clouds cut a starlit sky stretching quiet
from Fargo's brightest beacon lights—
a blue-white cry—to a chilling
May day's new-moon night.
I walk West Fargo's unsettled straddle
of its namesake neighbor's glow and of shrouded farmland.

My son is too tired to sleep even stroller-walking.
I secure our sleep rocking in a chair under a bathroom fan and
   light.

If you know Fargo, it's probably from a movie or its loosely
   spawned TV show,
but Fargo is an ideal anywhere shared
by every urban, suburban, near-rural
rooter in rich soil. Replace Fargo with your hometown or nearby.
Visit it for a familial pilgrimage;
mine is a gateway to a southwest-of-here homeland
homesteaded five and six generations ago in community with
   other ancestral German Russians.
Before I die, it'll have been two hundred years. My parents live
   there now.

Why return? Family; and a wilder part also,
for the wind-whispering leaves of trees lining vast fertile
fields or dense wildflowering grasses bearing grace,
despite defacing interstate and industry—necessary modernity
Because living is more than surrounding opportunity.

SPRING SNOWSTORM

Swirling snow of a spring storm
Obscures our farm yard
Cut and covered smooth by swarms
Of flakes freshly blown hard

By the same drifting northwest wind they blew in
On. A strong white yard light
Embodies the ice embers sideways falling
On the breeze like little leaves, and night's

Thick blanket blackens quick beyond
That light's reach. Mantled as by mist,
I pause to savor the pearling, and look long,
Past the fast entropic flurry, into darkness.

Hoarfrost covers trees and the ground at the Nies farm in North Dakota.

EARLY ICE

Frieze of frozen autumn,
Long hum of ancient gasps,
Leave me your shortened wisdom,
Give me your broken glass.

MINIWASHITU

Dakota Sioux tell of Miniwashitu—
"Water monster"—lurking in Missouri River depths.
It surfaces in spring, breaks through
The ice, and brings madness and death

To any who see it. Miniwashitu roars
Like cattle stampeding over grass
And dark-fisted thunder as it soars
Upstream smashing any impasse.

Its contours can be seen in the middle of the river
As flames of unbounded fire
Licking at the tide, obscured in silver
Mist and brackish water—never tired,

Never ceasing. Where do you sail,
Miniwashitu, what path do you take?
We hide from your approaching veil,
And tremble at your boiling wake.

Before death, madmen describe
The monster's saw-tooth vertebrae as sharp as teeth,
With fearsome limbs and claws. Its hide
Is covered by long red hair. It breathes

Thick through a snout like a buffalo's. One eye
Rests in its forehead and in its gaze the seers have seen
Fury, rage, and sadness compelling them to cry.
It is crowned by a white, curved horn of ivory.

Miniwashitu's image is the last any carry
As they look away—its fearless cruelty and grief;
None live through the insanity.
And Miniwashitu swims the river each spring.

PIKE FISHING

Neu's ditch filled with fish by flooding,
Notably Northern pike—trapped and hungry
From nearby lake to ditch. We used now-buried
Road as pier, casting steel-leadered spinning

Lures and reeling in—a quiet *click, click, whir.*
Pull bending pole, sudden line stop and fight to shore
Rattling tremors—fish sign, not common snag—careful to swerve
And rest fragile twenty-pound test, drawing the catch closer,
    closer.

Yellow-rimmed eyes glared from brackish waters
As a speckled brute fades in. We net then grab behind toothless
Gills while another extracts the lure with needle nose pliers.
Secure stringers are superior to five-gallon buckets

Because fish cannot jump out of them. Again cast, reel, snap, and
    fight—
A filled-limit day—and we shuttle our haul home
For close cleaning that never excludes all "Y" bones from the
    meat.
Fresh fried pike plate like walleye, except the bones.

INSPIRING LAND

To those clinging to a leaving hope that you
Can't wait to get away from your small North Dakota town,
I'd remind you that you're living on land that a man
Who had everything and pain proclaimed
He never would've been President without his Dakota get-away.
There's a wild mystery you might find, an inspiring
Thread of unspoiled passion that can sometimes look like
Black dirt as far as the eye can see,
Scalp-less rolling hills,
Violently turned buttes lording over fuzzy grass,
And, yes, lazy towns missing '50s heydays.
If you're willing to look for it, that Roosevelt-
Resurrection stuff might be smacking at your lips
Or kicking your ankles beneath insulated jeans.

THE BADLANDS

Back spine lined with ridged bridges
Over Little Missouri worry,
We marvel at your hurried buttes
Rising as chutes of earthen glory
Into mist and mystery, revealing history
Buried in their bellies.
Most folks rush headlong as always into horizons
Flush with skies surprised with nothing and everything.
How could they marvel?
But we are stunned lips, gun-hipped witnesses
To your magnificence!

Interstate 94 cuts through the badlands and Theodore Roosevelt National Park in North Dakota.

FARM SPRING DAY

Near-whispered warbles
Quiet coos
Distant driving din on a mile-away highway
Soft sunshine
Cold tinge left over from last night
And we're busy on a swing set
And sandbox
And trampoline
Giving goats respite
From our kid-coddling giggles

NORTH DAKOTA, SPRING - CHILDHOOD PAINTING BY THOMAS COLE

Beginning easy, earth and air emerge
From cavern gloom, forsaking frosty hold,
To carol infant anthems as new rivers
Flood the plain. Gone, great drifts of snow,

And in their place unwary budding sprigs—
Bur oak, boxelder, elm, and cottonwood—
Refill cadaver shelterbelts as rigs,
As soon as possible, sow intended food—

The farmer always keen the work gets done.
Yet Nature's humor rimes the feeble bine
When blizzards should have passed, and what was once
A hope is gone—the helpless lost to time.

Beware young sailor youth, your cherub's wings
Still close, a voyage grounds in fickle spring.

The Voyage of Life: Childhood, by Thomas Cole, 1842. Courtesy National Gallery of Art, Washington.

NORTH DAKOTA, SUMMER - YOUTH PAINTING BY THOMAS COLE

Explosive energy from morning dew
To afternoon, refulgent sun evades
Stochastic clouds while cattle graze and new
Construction breathes repair. The wind churns hay

In fields that farmers mow and rake and bunch
Till turning home as sunlight fades in calm
Descent—contrasting shades of plum and punch
Reflecting clear on glossy lakes, as long-

Belied ensemble passerines warble.
The spring-born calves cavort as wilder beasts
Prepare for night. "Museums have their marble—"
I say while gravel cracks beneath my feet.

Celestial visions sanction adolescence;
And held to boldly, antidote quiescence.

The Voyage of Life: Youth, by Thomas Cole, 1842. Courtesy National Gallery of Art, Washington.

NORTH DAKOTA, FALL - MANHOOD
PAINTING BY THOMAS COLE

Matured legumes and cereals, corn and beets,
Replete the combines, harvesters, and trucks
That farmers drive around the clock—machines
To lift and cut and thresh. And hunters pluck

Unwary game collecting scraps of chaff
To fatten up for southward flights or snow.
Communal celebrations—marked repasts
Of kuchen, sausage, sauerkraut, potatoes,

Halupsi, knoephla—gather socialites
And quiet countrymen alike to chew
Debated yarns and sports. The Northern Lights
Entrail the onyx sky in green and blue.

Delight of perfect sailing cheers, though rocks
May chop the course—as hope when all seems lost.

The Voyage of Life: Manhood, by Thomas Cole, 1842. Courtesy National Gallery of Art, Washington.

NORTH DAKOTA, WINTER - OLD AGE
PAINTING BY THOMAS COLE

Unflinching cold and wind hegemonize
The soil and glass the fallow grass and trees
In frost; and gelid lakes solidify
As stratus veils obscure with snow and sleet.

Cocooned emerging earnest hands grip pick
To open drinking-water tanks where parched,
Packed cattle slip—hooves rubbing on the drifts.
The sun's reflection blinds as sun dogs arc

Unchallenged rise across the sky, above
The dampened alabaster fields and pastures,
Beyond the circling blue. A labored trudge
To home again, where warming fire allures

Like parting clouds portending final port—
Eternal waters dark beyond the shore.

The Voyage of Life: Old Age, by Thomas Cole, 1842. Courtesy National
Gallery of Art, Washington.

HOMESTEAD

Tendril memories flash
As I turn down a gravel road
And sail highway speeds to our homestead,
Past a simile of tall shortgrasses
Swaying like waves in wind;
Long shelterbelt line marks field's end,
Which I've just to pass
To see another perpendicular,
And drive a rutted driveway
That needs blading
Through its veering curve from a blue tinned, white trimmed
  barn
And into a surrounded yard
by that barn, a granary, a house, and a quonset.

Foliage is season dependent
But I've always liked late spring
When blizzards are not still
Probable, though I've even seen snow in June.
Growing green trees like
Cottonwoods blacken with choral birds
Under blue sky dappled
By running clouds on warm breezes
Muddying winter-interred earth re-birthed.
This is our family's farm
When I return or see it in memory.

Freedom's seductive whisper crescendos
And urges action;
Untended ruin rises with the sun.
For its security, freedom requests exchange—
For roar of a tractor digging, discing, drilling;
For hammering, cutting, building, fixing;

For payoff of livestock tended and sold—
Its love song strung in chosen, running-farm work.

What our farm was—
Loyal labrador with shining coat lying full on the lawn,
Sauntering cows all named,
Cackling chickens,
Mischievous goats and contented sheep grazing—
I cannot forget.
If I want to return to boyhood,
Images are there
Finding power in familiar vestigial setting.
But I cannot return to past no longer living,
Even if I could forsake circumstance.
Our farm, which has always been our family's,
Hosts new experience—
Spring, summer, fall, and winter
In their cyclical washes—yet cradles viable
Seeds that can shift deep sediment.

I glide over earth and herb,
Feet-wetting grass, damp from yesterday's rain,
And drink thick air
Charmed by bugs and breezes over a low spot seasonally flooded
Behind homestead trees tall and old,
Planted necessarily for a farm deed years ago;
Diving into sod, generational connective roots
Anchor the arboreal monoliths objecting to endless prairie:
"Here, this family."

Clouds over a hayfield at the Nies farm in North Dakota.

SPRINGWELL - AN HOMAGE TO DYLAN THOMAS AND THE FAMILY HOMESTEAD

While once I worked between the worlds of who I was and would
Be, lilting over green grasses rustling exhalations,
Time watched me climb the hoary mornings
Gleaming white, in a blue
Dodge pickup, up ravines and hillocks
Stretched in wire or borderless—vast, empty feudal kingdoms
    farmer
Lords rule with machine-run sickles and plows, what ignoble
Nature I had passed too fast
When I charged for vain youth's chaining praise

Onto untamed rhythm-lands written before bloom, prairies
Preserved for millennia, though grazed differently from
Those glacier men melted away, who
Once thought they would listen
To meadowlarks as I could. And then
Departing, with Welsh Dylan's three-adjectives-a-penny
Lyrics rolling like stones in a rock picker, I knew that
I had cropped prerogative:
To preserve or embellish our farm.

And in marvelous months, I managed mangled memories
Towered in tires and steel tinsel until uncovering
Time-covered veins and vines communing
With those who sowed sod and
Slogged—bridge dialogue between me and
The deceased foundational denizens I descend from.
Bittersweet seasons blanch, green and golden dreams breathed
    once to
The wind sweeping all degrees
And whispering grassed and arbored bands,

Pitching potholed lands wildflower-strewn and stretching hot
   hours
Under summer sun to graft and game, as what youth remains
To sow and reap, steeped conventional
Traditions then and as
Seen now—boys to plow and plant and pick,
As my father did as his and his and his, girls to cook
And cope and clean, equally essential for reprieve from
Foreclosures and in keeping
Homestead deeds kept at the county seat.

Isn't that the prize? With eager apple eyes, I sized Time's
Holy offering by the knife, a life dichotomy: to
Carry an agrarian torch or
Not, faux dilemma fraught
With certainty—opportunity
Awaiting to again grace the lowing hills—and yet as
Much cut off forever from daily dust of a well-worn
Path spurned, I turned to other
Work, and that far afield. Yes, and though

I christened our farm with a proper name and selfsame sweat,
Like sires' by whose surname later local passersby will
Call the tree-sheltered unmanned lands, I
Saw but sought other than
My fathers' motherland and fruits; I
Am not unique, a truth clued by wilding leas belying
Slip dreams. Time wins eventually, though memories ease
Its turnings, and exhume the
Haunting heath's buried Dakota roots.

COTTONWOOD

Trees at the Nies farm in North Dakota.

It's not the wood that's cotton,
It's the seeds that float
Anywhere on a breeze, forgotten
As soon as seen (so small), yet hope

To root and carry on the race.
I built treehouses in them, which is
To say that my *dad* built them; I played
In them. There's not much you could miss

Like rough bark on a quick climb
Beyond short grasses summer-long,
Ripe, and jostling together in rhyme
While a big tree groans through its strong

Limbs and shoots, crown to roots,
Silk air stringing a thread. It's all
Nostalgic candy-sweet until you
Revisit it, standing unremarkable and tall.

It is as you remember—silver leaves
And a last yard-light-lit buoy before spook
Trees of a childhood evening, scared to sleep—
Yes, nothing more, and nothing less, too.

PLAIN ROADS

Section line road near the Nies farm in North Dakota.

Straight cincture grids—north-south,
east-west—cut clean troughs

In boundless land—mostly asphalt and gravel
New Deal make-work projects facilitating travel.

I assumed roads ran straight
Or mostly so—north-south, east-west—
Skirting only heady obstacles; now states
Away, I know winding ways. The depth

Of a good theory is its proof, and I have thought metaphor
Highways and county roads mirror a Great Plains life
Opinion—right or wrong, this way or that—

That looks simple from uptown or midtown or downtown
   skyscraper heights.

But of course roads are roads,
Nothing more or less.
They conduct the traveler
And facilitate commerce.
The views of farmers are direct,
Mirroring their landscape of life and death,
But they are no less sophisticated than their
Intricate infrastructure highway system,
No less inherently right or wrong about the world
Than those who do not live on its untamable prairie lands.

PRAIRIE CEMETERY

Scattered granite stones gouge
Manicured prairie meadow plotted
Carefully for coffined families
To rest—towering rightful
Henges conveying history cut
From sod. For some,
They are trivial; ancestral,
These scattered tombstones stand
Another way. And we
Peruse surnames parallel, savoring
What lives we lead.

STUFF I KNOW ABOUT WIND

When wind rushes just right, a guy can hear it whistle
through the grass
and trees
and sometimes just bounding over itself in open fields.

Wind speeds are always high, it seems, during the day
on the prairie
when a guy spends most time outside
working or what else. And it's constant, too,
though its gusts kick up dust and dirt.

If wind speeds get too high for too long,
a guy's skin starts to itch and doesn't stop
itching till it does without a guy even noticing.
It's called "windburn" but it doesn't last
like sunburn
or leave any cancerous side effects it seems
(at least a guy hopes it doesn't).
It's preventable too with a good shirt
and jeans
and a hat
and maybe some glasses—a guy's eyes can get dry from crying.

Wind farms have started to take their place
on agricultural land
and elevate skyward
so a guy can even see
their white-bladed peaks
during the day
when towers aren't flashing—
glowing red at night so as to help pilots so they don't run into the
    windmills.
But it still happens, not commonly but tragically,

68

that pilots do run into the windmills,
and it's all accidental
and expensive
and deadly.
A guy can run into things with a tractor
and still walk away.

Wind farms also kill a lot of birds, it seems,
but cooperatives and companies
keep building to harness
wind and make it useful
like what farmers used to do with well pumps and whatnot.
A guy gets so worked by the wind
that it can feel good to see it being worked.

THE RUSHING WIND

I have known the rushing wind
Like one with hand-plugged ears,
Like wind-borne tears,
Like afternoon grass wanting for rain.
There have been the headaches,
Birthdays,
Demands and hustles and whispers.
I've eaten when I'm hungry, and bathed in beauty,
Not just water, and hoped to taste new sunshine.
And the wind carries past all along
Like an oscillating pike or walleye
In brackish life—
All water is life.
And I've seen the wind and what it does
And felt it fill my lungs full of breath.
It carries the winter seeds to spring
And tills the harvest full.
I've grasped the wind's two trailing buckles
Like unlucky hair braids. I've risen unafraid
From her tongue lashings and reports.
She's slapped me like a whip
And kissed me blushing.
She is all and everything, a rushing
Knowledge, fickle yet older than my feet,
And even those can't root in the blood
My forebears are buried with, into the land
They poured themselves into.
Yes, she is the morning and evening,
My lying down and rising up,
Licking at my toes and cooling my hands.
But how much do I really know her?
I have not seen her sweep over the land,
Build to die and grow again.

I cannot trace her footsteps down mountains
Or see her prints on the yarrow and wormwood.
And yet, I can fly with her.
If I am prepared, she will fill my sails,
And I can fly with her.

EX-NORTH DAKOTANS MEETING

You could call us "ex-statriates," living like Hemingway
And Stein lost in generation and Parisian
Night life, for we have moved away from our home state
And growing-up family mountain

Trees like vines—cut free to find beyond North Dakota,
And not just Montana or Minnesota. It is of course
A divorce to barter childhood for a slice of
Bigger apples, but the exchange rewards

At least in satisfaction. So it is we meet in
Capitals of industry and government with thread-borne
Acknowledgment before beginning
To locate our old selves and form

Surprise connections. We critique and laud
Our Peace Garden, its politics and culture
And what we say defines a state, with broad
Strokes of hope and maybe even plans to return.

Part 3

PAUSE

MIST

Oh, turbid veil disguising tranquil lakes,
Rolling whispers of dew-drip mornings and captive nights,
Quieting calm in sunrise breaks,
Of sunsets in fading light—
You still, and then beyond,
Open your arms as I slip.

RAIN

Innocent, drops flicker onto grass,
Thicker blasts top canopies overhead:
The soul pulled from the sky.
I watch, listening to the glistening stead
Fresh with a word of life
To soak in, as long as it will last.

LIGHT RAIN

Light rain mists a blue morning.
My baby sleeps on me; we porch swing
And I listen with drooping eyes to
A neighbor dog yap and perching birds chat from power lines
Above a choral cricket rhyme.
Gray sky clouds the sun.
The ground is wet and grass stalks
Perch silver water drops.

BLACK DIAMONDS

Always the first time edge-overlook
Of black diamonds, or blacker,
Looks impossible to mortal eyes—
The gods rush
Heedless down Mount Olympus.
But slide, just slide into side-swishing small avalanches
And advance.

TREES ALONG THE BALTIMORE-WASHINGTON PARKWAY

The trees along the Baltimore-Washington Parkway
Sway as threaded pillows against an ashen sky. The day
Wakes above our car lights hemmed by the wooded walls
Paralleling our driving world like long halls
As we speed to work and play and home.
These trees are bones.

GREAT FALLS, OLMSTED ISLAND

Terrible foment—
    gurgling, churning, angry river
    pressed in caverns, over boulders,
    rushing tirelessly forward—
"Righteousness like a mighty stream"—
as we meander board-walked floodplains cleaned
    by now receded waters.
    I trail my son, careful father—
    wilderness exploring adventurers
together, consumed by the moment.

She, dedicated stroller spotter,
    and I turn to lead
    as he dawdles then runs laughing
    shouts, full of joy as we
walk islands straddled by a mighty torrent
roaring nearer. We are the innocent
    in a sun-filled day
    through downed trees and spray
    cooling the air as it evaporates.
"But let justice run down like water."

A VIEW OF GREAT FALLS

Oh mighty Potomac!
From thy granite, cubed perches
Jutting from earth as lively fingers,
I hold onto a tree
To breathe your holy offering, smoking
Under an altar of autumn sky,
Your clear blood greening-blue
In the deep channels.

A DRY RIVERBED

I have waited down a river run dry
of its rippling clean—its severed bed bent
by the floating rapid crash, knock, slurry
of stone and stone—bone-breathed current

disappeared for years' relentless heat.
I listened for wind chime rain as if elements could explain
searing weight of loss and cost in opportunity
deserted for a more fruitful plain.

I turned desolation to desolation
upon a hearth of windswept hopes,
ashes from bygone brilliant fires which heat and illumination
vanished, too. Yet I see dark clouds rising, and rain like smoke.

MAGNIFICENT AS A WAVE

Magnificent as a wave,
I rise above a rollicking ocean
Unabashed and unashamed
To roll through open

Lines to rise and break
And glass the constant shore.
I erode the wake
And all that comes before.

Buckling at my knees,
I gasp a foaming, final breath
In eternal retreat,
Triumph ushering death.

Fear the glory of my time!
Marvel at my mosaic legacies
Buried, as all, in rhyme
Like thunder rolling into sea.

OCEAN WAVES

You cannot imagine the waves;
They are there, corsair crashing graves
Of forever past and future days,
Imagined or not. Thought cannot
Ebb the flow, or the roll, roll, rolling sailor knots,
Fraught and fickle with furious rage.

PUSH-MOWED YARD

The beauty of a blade rips beneath a tearing turn
Of a gas motor gliding on plastic wheels. An American
Tradition—sweat-sown landscape lectern
Of suburban ideals and native plant caution—

Is a preen of proud monotony. And I step
From my part in the yard song, my hands green
And dry despite the rest.
This low herb blanket for earth is stark control and clean.

SPRING, DAWN

Growing light opaques
heavy fog of smoking dew
lying thick in dips,
parted from rolling crests—
as if I were looking
at vertebral grasslands
through squinted eyelids
nearly meeting.

I LIKE A SIMPLE THING SOMETIMES

I like a simple thing
Sometimes, an easy read
Without a mortal ending,
Like waving cottonwood trees
In prairie heartland breezes,
A broken something's mending,
Or a glass-like silver sea
Leaving the world to its worrying.

A pink flower from the author's garden.

DEAD-ALIVE CATS

Bare white clean rooms—
swept, washed, polished and smelling
of disinfectant—greeted me
as joyful harbingers of doom,

bare, empty, bare—each
more spartan than the last,
each dimmer, darker. The vast
laberynth drew and I knew it was inevitability

beckoning (*I know such things*)—door, black
tunnel straight, but disoriented, I fell
into either wall again and again. I felt
the path trail down, then up, then at

corridor's end, a light. Brightly blinded, smell
swept over me—dank body odor
and sweat—then I heard "Erwin Rudolf Josef Alexander,
we've been waiting." I could not tell

if I knew the greeter as my adjusting eyes were
greeted by two men—familiarly black and white
but I did not know them—nametagged "Death" and "Life."
A steel box-topped table stood lonely furniture

in the too bright and bare room. I
asked smart questions (*as I do*)
and they answered unheeding: "You
are here for that," gesturing to the bin. "Inside

lies a cat, dead or alive. You must choose
to open or leave closed the box."
I asked more smart questions (*as I would*). "Cause
and effect," they said. The silent steel-blue

cube sat still but seemed to draw
me in—*inevitability? Was the cat dead?*
Was it alive? I wish I knew. Instead,
I turned, retraced and left that quod

perhaps forever, perhaps to return again
and open the cat box in the bare room
(*I will have to choose*).
I emerged on Gammel Strand and kept

course around Slotsholmen, too
absorbed to appreciate Christianborg's beauty,
when I remembered plans with my hosts Werner and Niel,
and then thought only of that amid crisp sunshine.

.

PLAYGROUND DEER

Plastic and steel outline an escape
Above multi-colored rubber ground,
While the orange-red-yellow leaves
Of November dance and detach and disappear.
We're here, wherever here is, in minutes
Between skating lessons indoor,
As it's too warm for outdoor
Ice. When all of a sudden, our playgrounding
Focus shifts to a doe and passionate buck
With wide antlers projecting season.
He's hot on her and a river ridge hides their descent
Until, cross-bank, they rise amidst the thicker
Vegetation. Then another buck grunts his way before us
And holds us in his wild gaze
In pursuit of the two. My mind is all at once
Three hundred years before, in a cold wild—
No clearing, no playground: just deer and
Mad pursuit, the land and trees.
The laggard buck glides through water up
To his belly and bounds away.
A few minutes later, we're at the swings and
An airplane glides in, to land. And that
Vision of three hundred years ago spots me its
Modern adaptation.

PHEASANTS

We are a tribe because we say we are,
And what we did was take away from other tribes.
They live in our belly
Like brooms swept by dust storms
And the gliding pheasants of our past—
Magnificent, and elusive until the hunting dogs
Find or flush us, and then it's a reactive chance
That we might escape firepower beyond
Our pigeon-brained imaginations.

Credit, Gracie Welling.

HUNTING IS A BITTER KNOWLEDGE

Hunting is a bitter knowledge
Of insulated waders and pocket warmers camo-covered
From all humanity whispering their lives.
Waking elements set a waiting stage
Of determining gunshots.
At this point, a statistical ten percent will love or hate
What I have to say—half dreaming of so-close quarry,
Half seething that people play at being wolves.
Where are the wolves? They are not eating our pets and children;
We all admit a place for canine checks and balances.
What we disagree about is ethical, primal primacy,
If humanity's need to chase the wild is still beautiful;
We wrestle to forget and recapture who we once were.
And this is a bitter knowledge.

DEER HUNTING

Graceful, careful denizens—
Fixed on fattening and gleaning as much as possible
From dormant stalks and traces of hay—
Are ignorant I've fixed my scope's crosshairs on them.
I've not entirely followed their progression to this point—
My own enough—
But they've always been close as she's raised them,
Never always here but more or less near.

We have been brought together—
Though I actively stalked,
Carrying my Constitutional right
Of death or life, of death for life,
Primeval urge gnawing at my arms and legs—
But I haven't pulled the trigger yet;
I'm not sure I want to pull the trigger.
I've got one license.
They graze just there,
And I measure, think, and watch just here.

It's a buck I'm after;
I'm not picky, but it's a buck I'm after,
With a large spread of thick antlers
And a fat paunch and massive bulk.
There are one or two big, wily ones around,
Courting the local does and rasping trees in territorial show;
I've seen them; the neighbors have seen them.
I'm not picky, but it's one of those bucks I'm after.

Bureaucratic seasonal lines lifted,
I've been at it for two weeks.
It's easy to pull a trigger, but there are consequences;
A bullet is a series of events like dominoes

Depending on the strike—
Ineffective, mortal wound, instant death—
And if death: hauling the carcass home,
Preparing for butchering,
Hoisting high to skin, disembowel
And dry age a few days in a cool place.

We'll discuss saving the hide by tanning, but planning and
    executing
Some modern technique or better historic American Indian one
Are different things, so we'll leave it to the dogs
And it'll harden misshapen, shed, and disappear.
The meat is what we're after, mostly for hamburger or sausage—
Some make jerky, though planning and executing are different
    things—
Especially the tender backbone steaks
To butterfly and fry in butter with garlic and onions.

I lean again to the scope taking care not to rest my
Zygomatic bone on the circular, steel frame
To prevent a shooting-recoil black eye.
Still, doe and now-legal fodder fawns
Gather while I hunt—
Them if I weren't after a *buck*; I'm not picky, but I'm after a *buck*.
I lower my .270 and breathe crisp air that bites the back of my
    throat.
I rise to walk to the slough to hunt from the cattails,
Stretching my legs and warming my inevitably chilling toes.
And the deer, until now unaware I was here, scatter for a nearby
    belt of trees.

UNTITLED 216

Go ahead, write the stars
With Billy goat boldness
And puncture the ice—
Puncture the ice!—
Like a narwhal on speed.
Your spirit animal calls
A whispered name
Of a forgotten Greek god.
The spirits of spirits magma,
Ocean, liquefy, which is like saying
All matter that matters is floating
On ultimate pools of fire.
But we don't dream with our belly buttons
Except when we're hungry,
Just like nonsense can and can't make sense.

I HAVE STOOD AGAINST THE WIND

I have stood against the wind,
Bulwarked from what push would draw me in,
And secured homonyms of strength,
Never breaking beyond a prudent bend
To right again. Who can stand without restraint?
Will and art play lesser parts than preparation,
And rising cannot be inherited; no stand is given.
Yet, I have stood against the wind.

UNTITLED 112

Whispering willow,
I would not wallow
If what fingers
You welcome with
Would weigh me—
Only to sway on the wind,
Oh willow,
In your weeping leaves!

DEAD LEAVES

Golden green, dying from season's change,
It twists and silently groans
Detaching from the tree
From where it had grown—

Wafts and flutters on its way
Down to earth, its final resting place.
Where could it go from there once there,
Withered without grace,

Helpless and frail? It wasn't fortified
To save itself from death
Or to forever beg its mother
Tree for nourishing breath.

At its base of drink and life,
A leaf dies from unquenched thirst,
And no life appears in the bowel stem
To heal it—wretched, cursed—

Do I even hear the crunch it makes,
Its breaking bones
Among the cacophony of thousands
I trample on my way back home?

Part 4

STEEL

A MOMENT

"Don't write poetry about poetry, too much self-importance
and double-diving.
It's been done, like everything.
Leave poetry on poetry alone."
It's as true as the tomatoes I water, unconnected descendants
of seeds of seeds. Unimportant? *No*!
Today's catalysts all have yesterday in common, but *come on*,
this moment wouldn't be but for now.
It's self-contained importance, nothing if not the breath
of a thousand thousand cells to each capillary corner of our
    ringing souls,
all for today and, too, for tomorrow's to come.
The iron glide of a distant speed train, *chir-whir-chir* of night
    bugs,
whispering traffic rumble. A cool July night
creeps in at the edges of consciousness,
and just as a poem builds on others before, so, too, this night,
which is also at once like none before, and yet a metaphor.

A FINISHED GARDEN

A finished garden rests like the woodland breath
Of twisting cultivars. It is time and space and space between
A mash of mixing textures, of all colors and especially green,
Growing reservoir of hard won, trial-and-error success.

Gardening is progress and life at conception, ramifications
At their most concrete and furthest from.
How long can you live in the light of the sun?
And there it lies, like storms of micro-seasons.

BILLY GRAHAM

The story goes that studying-abroad
Wheaton students stopped at Epworth Old Rectory
To review where Wesleys were reared,
Famous Methodist evangelists.
Guide, Dr. Orr, missed one and
Retraced his steps till finding kneeling at a fireplace sill—
Once Wesley also had—
A humble man prayed, "Do it again."

Again an empty tent questioned if God had sent.
But with a "puff," the seats were not enough
To hold the Angelinos who came to hear
In clear Carolinian candor,
"Except you call on Christ..."
And thousands answered the call,
Including a former Olympian and hell survivor
Who was freed from his own hell.

"He'll wash away your sins..."
The celebrated crusader preached
To weeks of capacity city crowds under stadium lights,
To bush villagers and nomads by firelight;
The same simple message of hope for
Capitalists and communists, dregs and elites,
Across colors and cultures and creeds:
A true heart salve, redemptive Good News.

News evidenced the evangelist's exploits—
Expounding the Gospel to millions,
Counseling congressmen and senators and presidents,
Writing well-received, best-selling books—
And duly he was honorarily degreed and awarded

The highest medals, knighthoods, prizes, and finally a stately
wake.
"God has given us two hands, one to receive with and the other to
give with,"
He said, humbly accepting all, save Capitol cortège.

A FLOWER AND A CHURCH

We've eaten our pages to fill our bellies,
Burned our books to keep from freezing,
Drunk the liquid ink to quench our thirst.
And we walk like possessed spirits
With quick lips and our best pieces tucked
Beneath an arm while we scurry dark streets like rats
Looking for cats to eat us. An open door! We rush
Like madmen and women to the sliver of light
That opens for a fattened favor
And slams in our sallow artistic faces. One has a long nose
That catches the door, or rather it it, and she
Holds back tears. It's not broken. We move on.
An old church tolls bells. Why ring? There's little time
To mark the time, and daylight isn't for a day.
Ah, but I remember!
He and she do, too—soup and a bed. We cross the holy threshold
And leave our work at the altar, strangely,
Yet we walk well without our well-written weights.
The air is incensed. The halls echo with our feet stepping.
We wash in hot water that swells our parched
Limbs, water better, too, on the throat than ink.
But before I join for food and drink,
I walk a courtyard and see a flower in the night mist.
It is blue and delicate, how else describe that I'm weeping before
    it, weeping?
It is all beauty in petals strengthening itself
Against the gloom. Speaking startles and I whirl to find
A gentle voice asking me my name. My name!
He continues before I have to reveal my shame
In forgetting who I am; he tells me
A name doesn't matter here, that I am welcome.
I join the table but my mind is on the courtyard
Flower, and I can't decide why,

When conversation turns to its beauty and, yes, a rare specimen
Years in the planting and tendering and ramification: all
For an easy-breaking bud. I catch weary gardeners
Glowing in success, "test a truer salt than any," one says.
I can't stop bed-thoughts—one look! And I sneak away to pay
Last respects. It is more magnificent, emerging moon a perfect
    light
In which to behold. I must hold it; I do! I must take it away,
Dread-happiness sinks my stomach and I footfall
The halls again and gain the street.
I stop suddenly and whirl to hear that gentle voice as in the
    courtyard.
He asks what I'm doing and why. I don't speak.
He steps forward with my work and says I forgot it at the church
    altar.
I'm alone. My flower fades, cut-off.
My work is heavier than I remember.
I turn to walk away but stay,
And then plant the shrinking stalk.

I walk through that night as if it were each night;
Dead, alive, what came of that flower?
I've heard rumors of a garden.

Credit, Gracie Welling.

BELLS ON CHRISTMAS

I hear the bells on Christmas day
And curse whatever God may
    Be bellowing in their toll,
    Who cannot match my soul
For fire. The bells are forged in ice.

Can I escape the belfry's cry?
Though I stop my ears, though I deny
    The bell's ring,
    Yet they sing
Despite me. If only the clapper were vised

To its open mouth. Oh, how I rage—
Quiet, quiet—and kick the snow! If Grace
    Can see my fat
    Troubles, she laughs
At the infection as a gambler with dice.

I hopelessly focus on the still-ringing
Bells topping the church that I cling
    To in child memories,
    With salvation offerings
And Biblical heroes. *But I now have faith to fight*

Belief in a baby whose birth ushered in
Peace on earth, good-will to men!
    Then the snow cloud clears,
    And I find myself near
That holy steeple with a manger beneath in starlight.

And despite my fight, I am wrong, I see;
God is right. He is not dead nor does He sleep.
    No argument can
    Disprove Jesus as a man.
Do I believe him insane, liar, or the Christ?

GOOD FRIDAY

Silently,
You listened to false accusations
From people who did not know what they were doing—
Small-minded envisioners unaware their
Claims of Your messianic claims were true,
As you asserted. How outrage would have turned
To sorrowing pleas for forgiveness
If they had known as You knew.
But in wisdom, it had to be paradoxical,
And only through death did you choose to conquer death,
Unveiling new life for all humanity.

KNOW WHAT I THINK

I want you to know my opinion,
Because I have one
And I want you to know it.
It matters that Whoopi Goldberg didn't use
The right words,
That Canadian truckers are honking protests!
Yes, hear me roar the whole moon,
Listen to my shrill, iambic tune.

NIGHT EXPLOSIONS

Bursting air otherwise still—
Few cars caroling entries and exits—
Can't miss percussions remind of protests
Hastily readied, heartily joined.
Explosions upheave,
And there's no clearer prick of the moment—
Long building, long overdue—
While somewhere, patinated justice wakes;
And somewhere, she is put down.

PORTLAND PROTESTS

Portland protests except process
Favoring fever-pitched demonstrations,
Extrapolations that police brutality
Is rule, not exception, and that "the system" needs
Pyrotechnic reformation—
So seen by a federal agent. His endeavors to redress

Fires fires more, unmarked boogeyman
Bodysnatching innocent citizens into vans
Under orders from a petulant politician
Stormtrooping intolerant fascism
Onto our city streets, rubber bullets for spray paint cans
And arrests for passive resistance—so through the lens

Of a protester. Laser and gas blinded
Discernment eludes especially when we say again
And again the all-encompassing "they" did this,
Remiss to harvest shifting drift
Both right and wrong along partisan
Parallels, careful of mirror light lest we be reminded.

MOSQUES IN CHRISTCHURCH, MOSQUES IN ÜRÜMQI

On March 15, 2019, a lone gunman killed 49 people and wounded 48 others in shootings at two mosques in Christchurch, New Zealand. In northwestern China, the government has worked to forcibly "re-educate" and incorporate the Muslim Uighur people.

***

Faithful filled the Al Noor and Linwood
Mosques in Christchurch when a man,
One man—streaming deadly intent to uproot
Muslims from his colonized homeland—

Removed nearly fifty swiftly
From the Canterbury Plains—
Swaths of ages, never to breathe
Or be breathed into again.

International condemnation of white nationalism
Followed gun control headlines
And the world watched New Zealand's schisms
Heal as its citizenry grieved. Time's

Apothecary fingers can tune
Even broken threads; wounds gradually,
Mostly disappear. For weeks ubiquitous, news
Cameras trained for developments and we

Held interfaith night vigils for the victims,
Mourned with the mourners, eagerly
Awaited justice for the not-named him,
And then marched, marched along with history.

We hate the white-hate prompting murder
We have not quelled. At least we take note
And try to fight—furor
Spurring action—and in this, hope.

* * *

Faithful Uighur fill the Tartar
And Shaanxi Great Mosques to pray—
Grand religious centers of Ürümqi in northwestern
China—while surveilled to ensure they

Do not get out of line as some have. These
Historic Silk Road kings of Takla Makan oases
Slink from Big Brother Beijing's
Cameras as determined thought police

Have rounded up hundreds of thousands
For "re-education" while razing communities
In the shadow of the Tien Shan.
Where are the Turkic chatter-filled markets of Ürümqi,

Where the Muqam ensembles playing
Uighur songs, where the chance to live
Without persecutory fear? Extreme
Nationalism annihilates its victim citizens.

Is it more acceptable to blot out a way of life
Than life—horror gripping in ways rote
Suppression cannot, headlines but few, no night
Vigils, mourning, or justice—where is hope?

Terrible things can be done quickly;
They can be done slowly.
There are cries in the mosques and streets
In Christchurch, none in Ürümqi.

READER'S WORDS

Sweet serifs,
Capping direct demonstrations of twenty-six tools—
Semitic descendants more important mortar now than ever.
Letters, now often sans-serifed,
Are mine as I write, yours as you read;
Beauty may be in the beholder's eye,
But control is a bigger apple.

Mostly black,
Or some binary-coded black subset,
Letters crisply
Mark the page,
Mark the screen—
Bleeding,
Not bleeding—
Significant only in the reading.
They were my words;
They're yours now.

You know the rest of the story,
It's yours to create, after all.
Well-used tittles can titillate,
But arousal arises from within.
So I'll leave you here—
Narration and imagination's junction—
Promontory before uncharted seas.
My dinghy words
Would be of little use to you out there
In the face of self-determining gales.
Yet beware,
Erratic oceans quell.

FOR POSTERITY

Can you allay my fears when
What I read says the world is a hell
That we are handbasketing for our children?
Fired brimstone fields cannot swell

Electricity, space telescopes are useless for burying
The past, and politicians do not wipe away tears.
We may not intend to fill or spill and empty
Inheritance coffers unevenly across the years,

But our children play in stripped-open pits
To progress, and swim over bleached coral crowns of happiness
Buttressing idealized American scripts.
Yes, we, too, are contributing witnesses.

We can claim the time and to have saved or spent
For good or ill; but is it present gain to future detriment?

CLIMACTIC DEBATE

Dialectical, disaster and divine,
Our ruined sublime's ultimate line
Begins with a bite, then flight
From paradise, lost pyrite
Purity scattered on winds
Of hope to rest again in Elysium.
Industrial silver tarnishes as we dine
On too much food and wine
Mined, modeled and moved
Through generations—improved
Life attesting a natural blessing
Is what a body needs—
Without about a damn for land
And water whispering reprimand
As only sanguine sufferers can.
Shifting sands partisans
Parse and plan for a grand calamity
Facing humanity currently, or in so many
Years, when electric solar winds
Will recast carbon clouding heavens
On earth and capture collective convalescence
Of an essence critical for perspective—
No gloom without light or night without noon—
And carrying us, too,
On currents to a present perfect past;
Unless, instead, humanity is evolutionarily free to gas
And light a better future,
Secured and sustained by a minor
Iceberg tip of total bounty buried and booming
For ourselves and our inheritors, choosing
Pacifist conquerors to theoretically
Slip absolutely or not at all into paradoxy.

UNTITLED 109

At my age,
Leonardo Da Vinci was a master painter,
Alexander ruler of the known world.
They never had a good relationship with their fathers.
I cannot be what they were,
I will not achieve their heights of success;
But I have opportunity today
To be what they never had.

YOU CAN'T MAKE A POEM SING WITH "THINGS"

You can't make a poem sing with "things,"
Especially "somethings," or shine "sometimes."
It will or won't and it won't with generalities.
I've yet to meet an effective line

Launched by "someone" and finalized
"There, like that"—
Not that anyone (*you* see) would write like that. Also, hide
Not archaic language in poems, nor its style adapt

Or adopt. Too many antique words are pastiche odes
To dead poets whose poems have survived
But primary audiences have not. Yet, even old
"Things" are better than nondescript ply.

UNTITLED 228

Verge, cusp, precipice—
I stand above a turbid sea
Wracking in its eminence
Beyond what rock girds my feet.

What shall I fear to lose
In the thought of a spring?
Death rests in a tepid noose;
But Life bursts by diving.

LATE NIGHT WORDS

Into the dark hours we run
headlong like innocent nymphs whose hieroglyphs
burn in the morning sun.

Drag away the curtain of our youth
and draw with knives into our bleeding hides
what words we won't escape, the truth

chasing us downstairs into a basement
of afternoon dreams, when we wake, and in an evening take
a breath before we tire to embarrassment

and dwindle in the shade.
Yes, we are men and women of art, of our pens,
dying on living edges of a blade.

MAY YOUR MEMORIES BE YOURS

And not stolen by a screen's glare
Innocently given, not knowing
Its due—precious lives played
To no watching audience,
Appreciative only of information
Not affecting like the in-front-of-your-eyes maturation
Only showing once.

NAP TIME HERE

Contented drowsiness, end-of-long-day cool sheets
Tucking between my legs and belly,
Peanut butter-jelly sweetness of life well lived,
Six month-old daughter asleep in my arm's crook;
There are potato problems in a next room.
But we are in *this* room.

HOW OLSON THE OWL FOUND FRIENDSHIP

Credit, Gracie Welling.

Olson the owl lived in a big oak tree hollow
That afforded a perfect perch for micing,
For mice are an owl's favorite snack to swallow,
Like chocolate cake with chocolate icing.

He was old and happy with his comfy life,
But friendless and grouchy to any other
Owl. "Too true, mine is mine!" he'd say; "I
Don't care to share, not even if with my mother."

Olson's unfriendliness stemmed from greed
And a misunderstanding of the woods,
Believing too many fight for a share of its scarcity
And that an owl has to claim its proper goods.

One day, as he was busy sleeping,
Olson woke to knocking; and investigating
Found two little owls trying to beak-climb his tree.
He scolded, "Who said a beak's for climbing?"

The little owls awed. "Who are you?"
Olson rose and fluffed his brown-gray-white
Feathers and said, "Shoo."
The little owls asked, "Can you help us climb right?"

Olson shook his head, which for an owl can be quite a thing
Because they can turn their necks almost completely
Round. "Fly!" He spread his wings and soundlessly
Flew, then returned. "Not your beaks, use your wings."

The little owl skeptics swallowed hard,
Then one and the other flapped and jumped
Into the sky, lifted, and flew far
Above the ground. Olson "humphed!"

"Who would've known?" they said, landing.
Olson said they could scat, and returned to bed.
But before he fell asleep, he heard the owls talking:
They had no place to go; they hadn't fed.

And Olson felt sorry for the owlets. "You should hunt mice.
They're easy to see from my tree." He shuffled space
And they joined him to watch the woods, all with yellow eyes.
Flash, flash! The little owls dove to talon-grab gray

Mice. They allocated Olson a first thankful beakful.
He wondered, maybe a forest furnishes enough food
For more than one owl? "Humph!" Most owls are nocturnal—
asleep by day, awake by night—and their pursuits

Had lasted long. Olson yawned. "You should find
Your own homes." The little owls said "certainly"
And departed for other trees, but they returned after a short time.
Olson scowled. "Whoever heard of owls that can't sleep?"

"Roosts are hard to find," they said. Olson sighed then soared
Among the trees, finding both owls good roosts.
Finished, he returned home, exhausted to his core.
He slept and overslept the night, finally waking to a new

Day. He exclaimed, he pouted, he rumbled, he shouted;
He was hungry. But as he readied for a day hunt, he looked
Down and saw dinner. "How did —?"
The little owls had left him food! He ate and took

Another rest and that night felt better than ever.
He met the owls and thanked them for their gift.
Then they hunted, a tradition they continue together.
And that is how Olson the owl found friendship.

COBWEBS OF CHILDHOOD

Cobwebs of childhood rue,
Linger long after easy-laugh echoes die,
Past pictures of a past
When we grew fast
Forever, until Time surprised
Us with perspective for our youth.

DO NOT FORSAKE SMALL DAYS

Do not forsake small days,
When efforts seem in vain
And careful words cascade
And disappear "never again

To be seen." Small streams
Cut great canyons, deep and wide.
Who knows, but today's trivialities
Might bombshell tomorrow's surprise?

POTTY TRAINING

Potty training is a dichotomy
Because you see your kids at their best and worst—
Get your hands in their worst, in all the worst anyone could
    conjure—
But you witness the pride of teaching, instilling, habit-forming
A lifetime of functional second nature.

AFTER BATH SWINGING

My youngest boy shouts "please!" like Captain Hook in Disney's
    Peter Pan
Shouts to his henchman Smee at the end of the Tiger Lily rescue
    scene.
Is he assuming I'm going to say "no?"
But I'm already reaching for the blanket I'll wrap
Him and my oldest in to swing around safely
In our bedroom. It's a tradition that started a week ago as a
    towel-swing.
How quickly traditions and habits grow,
And how powerful their realization in giggling
Drawls as both fly above the floor and then into bed
And then into pajamas and then into sleep.

BEFORE-BED POEMS

Evening pearls,
Slip my sight
To inward eyes
Where wayward daffodils

Dance, where
Music against music
Voices hope infused with
Truth. And I will dare

To dream your light,
To clam your secrets
And breathe them
Through, and through the night.

SLEEP WAKING

Flashing fat-cheeked, middle-of-the-night sleep
smiles, I wish I weren't too tired to return
one, running instead back to sleep
with hardly time to appreciate the singular
pearls he jubilates, barely awake
and only briefly
before we both again take
a dive into dreams.

LOVE MOVES

Love is a four letter word
Much better seen than heard
Through the bitter black smoke
Of hard grief and dashed hopes—
A ripple chord of strength
Without measure or length
For depth
And eternal breadth.
It pierces a thousand dark nights
To save shipwrecks by its light.
Do not merely speak L-O-V-E's name;
It requires action to explain.

MY WIFE IS ALL OF A THOUSAND STORIES

My wife is all of a thousand stories
unveiling like winded chimes
of a sunrise morning,
and soft wool: *peace.*
She is a chord of mountain roots
distilling snow life and avalanching down its
beautiful face to warring waves
of boundless prairie grasses ripening hot in the sun, setting place:
    memory.
And though I were to dive beneath her coral
waves of warm currents carrying
fresh fruit to the blossom,
I would have only begun to listen
to her campfire praises
carrying under blanket stars
of a spotted sky: *spirit.*

THE LOVE POEMS I COULD NEVER WRITE

The love poems I could never write
Sing in the eyes of my wife.

ASTEROID LIVES

Once, a boy met a girl,
And they danced the moon
Through to sunrise,
To their surprise,
As they were just a boy and girl.

How can two move the moon?
Yet, there at dawn,
They on the world's edge
Were, it seemed, its only song.

Scoff from your skeptic seat,
Or coo, if you will.
There are some songs that can't be joined
Or beat;
There are asteroid lives
When first they meet.

AN ELEGY

It may be that the Almighty's first creative words were songs,
And that the heavens were fashioned as a hymn
Of expounding breath—the morning stars and sons of God
    rejoicing along
With all of new-stretched Time. And that is how we begin,

As image-bearing caretakers a little lower than angels
And our whole beings a melody of praise. Even the rocks
Cry out, composed of whirring symphonies of universal
Building blocks. Read sometime of atomic frequencies and clocks

Functioning to the tunes of tireless trills.
Is it any wonder why God's eye is on the sparrow?
And how much greater He esteems us! We will
Sing; the question is, *will* we? And though

We gather to mourn the loss of such a voice—our altar-called
Beloved has gone before us to real glory—
He still sings, and even truer for heavenly halls.
He does not know but bliss. Yet, it is good to cry our memories

While we celebrate his life; it is O.K. to stand at his grave and
    weep.
We are human, after all, and we swim the wake
Of every breath. But the end of life is not death. And we
Have and carry the best of bonds that will never rust or break.

www.ingramcontent.com/pod-product-compliance
Lightning Source LLC
Chambersburg PA
CBHW060353090426
42734CB00011B/2122